294.544   Strano, Anthony
STR
        Seeking silence

Check For ① CD before discharging

DATE DUE

SEEKING SILENCE

SEEKING SILENCE

Exploring and Practicing the Spirituality of Silence

ANTHONY STRANO

STERLING ETHOS
New York

STERLING ETHOS
New York
An Imprint of Sterling Publishing
387 Park Avenue South
New York, NY 10016

ISBN 978-1-4027-8416-3 (Hardcover)
ISBN 978-1-4027-8909-0 (ebook)

Library of Congress Cataloging-in-Publication Data

Strano, Anthony, 1951-
Seeking silence : exploring and practicing the spirituality of silence / Anthony Strano.
p. cm.
Includes bibliographical references (p.   ) and index.
ISBN 978-1-4027-8416-3 (hardcover and cd : alk. paper) 1. Silence--Religious aspects--Brahmakumari. 2. Spiritual life--Brahmakumari . 3. Brahmakumari--Doctrines. I. Title.
BL1274.245.S77 2011
294.5'44--dc22
                                        2010036655

Distributed in Canada by Sterling Publishing
c/o Canadian Manda Group, 165 Dufferin Street
Toronto, Ontario, Canada M6K 3H6
Distributed in the United Kingdom by GMC Distribution Services
Castle Place, 166 High Street, Lewes, East Sussex, England BN7 1XU
Distributed in Australia by Capricorn Link (Australia) Pty. Ltd.
P.O. Box 704, Windsor, NSW 2756, Australia

For information about custom editions, special sales, and premium and corporate purchases, please contact Sterling Special Sales at 800-805-5489 or specialsales@sterlingpublishing.com.

Manufactured in the United States of America

2 4 6 8 10 9 7 5 3 1

ᘓ Contents ᘖ

Preface

REFLECTION
What is the difference between peace and silence?
Peace is something we want inside. Silence is when we leave
the world outside, to go inside. When we go inside we are
able to find the peace that we have lost.

—Dadi Janki

Just as other forms of pollution have reached an extreme state in the twenty-first century, so too 'noise pollution' is extreme at the moment. So today, more than ever, we need to experiment with the power of silence and experience the many ways in which it can heal body, mind and soul. Wherever you are in the world, you will be bombarded by noise. Even if you go to a very quiet place—a wonderful beach, for example, far away from civilisation—you will be surrounded by noise. For even if there is no noise outside, you will probably be experiencing a great deal of inner noise!

When we are surrounded by a world of sound, we are not always aware of all the noise we generate inside our minds. But when we find a quiet space, away from exterior sounds, we are able to become more aware of the noise—that insensate constant chattering—going on inside. Maybe at night when you are trying to go to sleep, instead of letting the mind become quiet and experience that rest that can bring refreshment, you become aware of all the noise inside you. At times such as this, the mind moves very quickly, revisiting not just the experiences of the day just past, but also replaying scenes that took place during the week or even last year. How do we deal with all this mind-noise? Is it even possible to deal with it, or do we have to accept it as part of human life?

This book explains why we *can* find inner peace and offers simple techniques to guide you towards it. It demonstrates how, by practicing silence, we can acquire the awareness to move beyond the confusing, unpredictable and artificial experiences of modern life to find an inner system of reference that offers complete and long-lasting well being both to individuals and to society as a whole.

Silence opens up a dialogue with the self and a dialogue with God; both are essential if we are to find the spiritual direction we need to live fulfilling lives. Silence helps us to tap into the neglected spiritual reality of the self—an invisible but dynamic reality that flows inside each one of us. Silence nourishes within us a quiet courage and optimism. In the light of silence, we experience the power of the invisible spirit within and can create a life based on truth.

In this book, I share with you my personal experiences of practicing active, inner silence, and suggest exercises that will help you to enjoy the many benefits that silence can bring. Each chapter introduces attitudes, thoughts, techniques and teachings that can help you to explore and practice silence. Scattered throughout the chapters of the book you will also discover practical tools for seeking silence, which include:

REFLECTIONS: sayings from a sage or a thought from the author to focus your contemplation on aspects of silence.

PEACEFUL THOUGHTS: particular thoughts that allow the mind to quieten and begin to discover silence.

TAKE A MOMENT: suggested practices to help you explore the theme of the chapter and deepen your personal insight.

I hope this book will be helpful to everyone searching for a deeper understanding of spirituality as well as readers who wish to bring the healing power of silence into their lives. When we decide to embark on a spiritual journey, it is always helpful to have an example to follow or a model to learn from. I have learned many things from the example of the Indian teacher Brahma Baba, whose work began in the mid-1930s. Through his deep commitment to the divine and to the divine task of renewing and uplifting human consciousness, he became the embodiment of creative spiritual silence. A group of young women, whom Brahma Baba spiritually sustained and guided, provided the foundation for what has become the Brahma Kumaris World Spiritual University, and the teachings of these esteemed elder sisters have inspired this book through their work with Baba's principles of respect, kindness, acceptance and belonging. They include Dadi Janki, the Administrative Head of the worldwide Brahma Kumaris Spiritual University. There are also thoughts scattered throughout the chapters from Jayantiben and Sister Sudesh.

REFLECTION

*Time is such that every second, every moment, every day and
every season is filled with wondrous opportunities.
Each day is a jar filled with seeds of possibilities and I can
plant any aim, any wish, any destiny I choose.
However, the jars cannot be known until I become still and click out of my
mundane consciousness, open my eyes and recognise that the opportunity is
there, and in fact, has always been there—but I did not recognise it or, if I
did, I neither decided nor acted on it.
Every day brings a renewal of opportunities. This is the blessing of time.
The jars are waiting to be opened and the seeds are waiting to be planted.*

Introduction to Silence:

Some Historical Perspectives

Reflection
There is always a way.
The light of silence guides that way.

THE IMPULSE TO CREATE AN INNER SPACE OF STILLNESS and quiet has always existed. We need to make use of this impulse if we are to make any pioneering leap in progress toward self-enlightenment or any other human achievement. We have a natural attraction to a state of deep concentration, to dropping into the depths of a particular awareness or understanding. In its purest form, silence is not a technical exercise (although we may have to begin our relationship with silence in this way); it is an irresistible pull toward a pure experience of the truth of what we are concentrating on—which may be God, an idea, a principle, or perhaps some element of the self.

A person who feels the attraction of concentration and inner silence knows that experiencing truth is the highest form of knowledge. When the mind is uncluttered by the desire to prove, to claim, or to display, everything becomes clear in silence, in that stillness of the mind and heart. Then, at the right moment, we experience a creative flow toward a new and clear perception. This moment of epiphany comes by itself; it is not something we can calculate or maneuver toward.

When the poet W. B. Yeats was asked how he had written one of his most famous poems, he replied that though he had a pencil and paper, the poem wrote itself; he just happened to be there. Indeed, when the mind is absorbed in stillness and silence, and when the ego is quieted, a space inside forms from which creative thought is born and can be effortlessly expressed.

In silence, the true creator goes beyond "I" and "my," allowing "the other" to do the inspiring and guiding. Of course, this creative process is clearly linked to conscious processes that have already taken place and become merged in the subconscious; but then a trigger—such as a scene, a word, a sound, or a person—suddenly generates a flow of fresh insight. In the introduction to Fritjof Capra's *The Tao of Physics*, the author tells of a similar experience. Having long researched different aspects of physics, he went on a holiday near the sea just to relax. While quietly sitting at the seaside there, he experienced a vision of atoms and molecules dancing in beautiful symmetry and harmonious rhythm. He was mesmerized. The ancient Hindu god Nataraj, the Lord of the Dance, came to his mind. The movements of the atoms and molecules were rhythmic, flowing and ebbing in a dance of order and balance. It seemed to him at that moment that the whole universe moved constantly in this way, like the rhythmic limbs of the divine Nataraj. This revelation, both as an experience and as a perspective of knowledge, inspired his future research and writings.

Knowing the Truth

Leaving the shores of Capra's physics and journeying back a few thousand years to ancient Greece, we meet Pythagoras, one of the first physicists and someone who also had mystical experiences of scientific truths. Pythagoras's desire to know was not just a wish to understand intellectually the divine laws governing nature and the cosmos; equally important, for him, was to *experience* those laws. He regarded this experience as essential for a scientist. He founded a school in which students learned certain aspects of science (especially mathematics) by means of a system of understanding that was philosophical, spiritual, and practical. Those who wished to become his pupils were required to undergo a very deep preparation. In addition to a vegetarian diet, celibacy, and a number of other strict disciplines, on first entering the school they were required to adhere to a two-year period (some say a five- or even seven-year period) of complete silence. The aim was to clean from their minds all the desires and conditioning that would hinder them from comprehending and receiving truth. Pythagoras believed that a pure state of mind was a prerequisite for any researcher of truth and that silence was a vital tool in the creation of this purity of mind and character. For Pythagoras, integrity was even more important than intellectual prowess.

While the school's learning and research activities did include mental work and discussion, the students also contemplated aspects of geometry and mathematics because Pythagoras had taught them that numbers, points, and lines were aspects of divine truth. For example, they believed that zero holds the greatest purity because it always adds value to a number, whereas it cannot be added to or subtracted from as a value in its own right; it is whole and complete. The Divine Architect of Pythagoras's harmonious cosmos was accessible only through a silent alignment of a "clean" mind. The aim of his research and teaching was to achieve this aligning experience, which he believed would open the consciousness to understand reality better. The validity of this method is echoed in the words of Albert Einstein, who said, "I hold it true that pure thought can grasp reality, as the ancients dreamed."

Touching reality can be experienced in a moment when "something clicks"—one of those "Aha!" moments. In ancient Greece, there lived another famous mathematician, Archimedes. He experienced one of his great discoveries while taking a break from his labors. Indeed, after much thinking about weights and measures, Archimedes was relaxing in a bath. In a state of peaceful calmness, he noticed that his body was displacing a certain amount of water. Suddenly he got it! He understood in that "Aha!" flash. So overwhelmed was he by this experience that Archimedes jumped out of the bath and, as the story goes, forgetting that he was naked, ran through the streets shouting, "Eureka! Eureka!" ("I have found it!") He had discovered the law of buoyancy.

Faith in Silence

Religious leaders have also been renowned for spending long periods in silence. Muhammad contemplated in a cave for many consecutive days, whereupon the archangel Gabriel dictated the Koran to him; Buddha, in deep silent meditation under the banyan tree, defeated the seductive temptations of the demon Mara and emerged enlightened; Christ spent forty days of silence in the desert, overcoming Satan and strengthening his resolve to fulfill his Father's wishes.

Further down the centuries, we stop in medieval Italy. At this time, the people were divided by factions—both religious and political—and Roman Catholicism had, to some extent, become a collection of showy rituals, offering little solace to a people in need of a nourishing Christianity. Stories handed down from the time tell of Saint Francis of Assisi spending time in solitude and silence on his beloved mountain, Mount Alverna. Here he found himself filled with an overwhelming desire to follow in Christ's footsteps. In prayer, he implored that he might experience what Christ had experienced, and immediately stigmata began to appear: marks of nails in his hands and feet and an open wound on his right side.

In other moments of silence, Francis spent time in nature, feeling the wonder and love of God as Father and Creator—joyous feelings were rare in the war-torn Italy of that time. He felt the inclusiveness of the whole of creation, to the point where he saw the birds, the flowers, and even the sun and the moon as his brothers and sisters. Francis's example

4

became a great inspiration for thousands seeking to review and remodel their lives on original Christian principles of love and peace.

Touching down in medieval England, we find a nun, Julian of Norwich, living in solitude while contemplating the love of God. She experienced God not just as the Creator Father but also as the Divine Mother. Her experiences gave her a feeling of complete trust in God and in life. No matter what happened, she wrote, "All will be well." She believed this for herself and also for others. Julian was one of the first recorded people in the West to experience God as "the Mother" and comforter. The aspect of God that is sweetness and forgiveness can clearly be seen and felt in her words.

The levels of silence are many, but for each of us, whoever and wherever we are, silence brings peace to our minds and purpose to our lives. It is the greatest necessity and the greatest healer. We can learn how to integrate silence into our lives simply by being quiet from time to time during the day. Silence begins with a thought, and since everyone thinks, anyone can reshape his or her thinking to discover the treasures of quietness, which are so many and so wonderful. The following chapters will show you how.

PEACEFUL THOUGHT
In this place of peace and stillness
I am now free from all that bound me to empty
routines and a meaningless lifestyle.
All is well.

❧ 1 ❧

STOP . . . and take a breath

PEACEFUL THOUGHT

Every day there's the same mind chatter, the same rush of words,
the same stressed reactions, the same put-downs (of myself and others),
the same this . . . the same that.
"Take a break!" I urge myself, "Put the thought brakes on!
Stop! Just for a moment—one moment of calm."
Mmm . . . definitely time for a change—for everyone's sake!

WHAT'S THE BIG APPEAL OF SILENCE, THEN? you might ask. Noise is great—indeed, it's essential if we're going to enjoy life. Noise is part of the fun of socializing—chatting over a drink, gossiping around the water cooler—and essential to our leisure time—watching TV, playing video games, listening to music. How else do you expect us to have fun or relax?

That we enjoy such noisy activities shows just how far we have become divorced from our spiritual lives. We might picture such activities as a labyrinth of distraction full of confusing passageways that initially seem to promise happiness and fulfillment but ultimately turn out to be dead ends. As we explore these restricted passageways one by one, we find that our ability to enjoy life also becomes blocked. Gradually, we resign ourselves to living superficially and haphazardly—in a noisy way—so as to avoid or camouflage the unsettling reality of such personal emptiness.

The Silent Truth

Most of us feel some emptiness within, or a neediness or discontent, and yet we don't realize that what we are hungering for is the experience of inner silence. This inner silence is able to fill and satisfy us, giving us the inner strength and ability to heal ourselves by putting us in touch with the real meaning of life. Deep within, we all remember the meaning of life. We could think of these sketchy memories as the few remaining strands of a thread of life. Sometimes, little everyday situations—such as an unexpected moment of silence during a busy day—jerk this strand, stirring up an innate feeling that reminds us, "I am something more. I can be something else."

This tug of the thread kindles a desire to search, to find out what that "something more . . . something else" is. Perhaps that is why you picked up this book. A hope stirs deep within—the thought that we are not bound by anyone or any situation. It reminds us of what we are at core—not what we are as a parent, spouse, or child, or because of a job or special talent, but what we are because each of us is a self that lies beyond the social, physical, and emotional realms. We might think of it as a point of eternity—a point of unique spirit within the universe, which is eternally me.

So the inexplicable pull of that thread is accompanied by the feeling that "there is something I must reach, something I must know, and (even more important) something I must *be*." Now, we ask, how can I catch hold of this thread that will guide me and enable me to clearly see the difference between the dead end of the noisy world and the open door of real life? "Simple," a little voice whispers. "It seems difficult and laborious, but it's not; it's as easy as stopping for a moment and becoming silent." Try this simple exercise in silence to see how easy it can be to find your own thread:

Take a Moment . . . to stop and be silent

1. Take a moment—or two, or three—whenever you remember just to stop. Be still and silent.

2. Sense the quietness of that moment, and visualize yourself stepping into an ocean of calm. Submerge your whole being in the quiet waters.

3. As the waves of that calm ebb and flow, begin to unburden yourself. Slip into a place of no thinking, and become completely still.

4. Now, in that stillness, become aware of your "original" self. This is the real, true you. Let it appear quietly but brilliantly.

5. After some moments, emerge from the still waters and try to retain an awareness of the true you as you go back to your everyday affairs.

Where to Stop

You can try this exercise in many places—the world is filled with opportunities to stop. You might settle into a peaceful spot in nature, choose a garden bench on a moonlit evening, or find a quiet corner of a room. Or you might choose to spend time in a more formal place of retreat, where you can share silence with others on the spiritual path. Wherever you choose to start being silent, in that complete calm, you will find that the ancient memory starts to stir, and then, as your attention becomes more and more concentrated, you remember. What do you remember or experience? An original state of being, which is serene and complete. You might find yourself thinking, "At last; this is me!" It's like awakening from a deep sleep. In this state of quiet wakefulness, the mind stops thinking, no words can be spoken, and the ears do not function. There is just the happiness of discovering yourself through silence.

PEACEFUL THOUGHT
It is not so difficult.
All I have to do is give myself permission to stop—to stop for just a moment
in this hectic spinning called life.

❦ 2 ❧

TAKE CONTROL . . . be the boss
of that noisy mind

REFLECTION

When I learned to find that quiet space within myself, the space in which I am able to experience that inner silence, I realized how hungry I was for it. How much I had missed it and needed it!

—Jayantiben

THE STARTING POINT OF THE HEALING POWER OF SILENCE is our thoughts. Thoughts are extremely powerful; indeed, since we speak and act according to the quality of our thoughts, they create the world around us. Generally each of us has about thirty-six thousand thoughts per day. Some days there are many more—as the day gets more and more tense, there might be thirty-six thousand thoughts an hour. How fast the mind works! It's like a machine. But we've forgotten that we are in charge of this machine; we can determine the speed with which it moves and the direction it takes. Yes, we can decide in which direction the thoughts go, and we can determine the quality and speed of those thoughts, too.

Mostly, we're not aware of this, and so the machine is taken over by external influences. We see or hear something or someone, and we react, forgetting that we have independence and choice. No matter what is going on outside, we can choose our thoughts, and the more we understand and practice this understanding, the easier it becomes to remain calm, understand what we need to do, and act accordingly. This thought-control process begins with silence. When you practice silence, you can transform yourself from the "headless chicken" constantly reacting inappropriately, to someone who is master of his or her thoughts. This doesn't take months to achieve—it can happen in the space of a day! When you master your thoughts, you can start to create beautiful, powerful, and pure thoughts, and you can also create the space between those thoughts that allows you to tap into the healing power of your own inner silence.

How to Begin

But what's the most effective way to begin to control the mind when it's jumping around, thought thumping against thought, as it strives to do just as it desires? We can try consciously to calm the mind, encouraging it to be quieter, but since thinking is so closely linked to long-held habits and emotions, the mind finds it hard to "listen" and gaily continues its merry-go-round existence.

The inner argument between the self and its mind was a topic that preoccupied Brahma Baba, the founder of the Brahma Kumaris World Spiritual University, as he started out on his path of spiritual realization and service. He wrote about the struggle to become the boss of his noisy mind, and it reads like a manifesto for all of us setting out to live quieter, less stressed, better lives. His key was to "quarantine" the mind with silence for twenty minutes every morning and evening. At the end of this chapter, you will find an exercise that will help you, too, to become the boss of your own noisy mind.

SELF: Mind, what are you doing now? I do not wish to think the things you put in my head. You purposely do the opposite of what I want:

I decide to be peaceful; you accelerate the stress.

I commit to being sweeter; you pour out a ton of salt.

I concentrate on the goodness of others; you hang up their dirty laundry.

I try to live in the present; you push me into the past!

Are you working with me? Tell me honestly.

Mind, you have a mind of your own, but there cannot be two minds in one head.

So make up your mind, O Prince, to be my faithful friend, and stop making alliances with my rebellious ministers—especially Ego, Anger, and Complaint; they are constantly trying to overthrow me, trying to rob me of my peace, my respect, and my contentment. . . .

Okay, Mind! Listen carefully. These words will not confuse you; they are quite clear!

From today, I INSIST *that you will not do what you like, when and how you like.*

You have heard this before?

But this time I am determined. There is no point in laughing. Today it is different. . . .

From today, every morning for twenty minutes, and every evening for another twenty minutes, I will quarantine you—in silence.

Don't laugh! You do not feel sick, you say?

But you are, and I will put you in quarantine every day.

You have to see it to believe it . . . ? You don't stop being sarcastic, do you?

The quarantine of silence will be very useful for you, Mind.

By practicing silence, we too can begin to take control over the mind and govern its rebellious thoughts. The mind doesn't easily accept being reined in, but gradually, with patience and perseverance, it becomes cooperative. Then we discover personal balance and peace. Start by trying this simple exercise in the morning, before heading out into the world:

Take a Moment . . . to return to quiet

1. Each morning, before beginning your day, stop for a moment or two and become still and silent; then fill your mind with quietness and peace. Do this with a loving attitude. During the day, this quietness and peace will transform into clarity and attentiveness.

2. As you travel through your day, watch how your mind loses this quietness and becomes full of haste, reacting

with twists, jumps, and spins at any moment, in any place, and with anyone. Watch how it insists and bullies you.

3. When you notice the mind rebelling in this way, allow yourself to stop and replenish your quietness and peace. Do this as often as you wish or need. It may take just a second of silence for you to regain your equanimity, or it may take a minute or two. By returning to quietness and remembering your original peace, you will quickly regain your clarity and attentiveness.

4. As you come back into the everyday world, try to retain some awareness of calmness and peace.

REFLECTION

So, Mind, your revolutionary days are over.
And, furthermore, every hour, for just a minute, I'll check on
what you are doing, where you are going.

—Brahma Baba

∞ 3 ∞

START . . . face the challenge
of the first step

REFLECTION
Let us allow ourselves to become our own spiritual leader.
Let our feelings be filled with love.

—Dadi Janki

NOW THAT YOU BETTER UNDERSTAND THE VALUE OF SILENCE and appreciate its ability to recharge and renew, you might choose to set out on a quest to make silence an integral part of your life. That's a brave decision. When you begin to leave behind habitual routines and reorient yourself, inevitably the mind roundly rejects your venture and embarks on a campaign to seek distraction and pursue the unnecessary: "Not now! Later," it will say; "This spiritual stuff is a luxury pursuit! It's not real! There's no time for this now!"

When we make any decision, reactions arise that are both conscious and unconscious. So even as we consciously seek change and welcome its effects, the unconscious mind resists it tooth and nail. How can we deal with this? Make a decision clearly and firmly; then keep to it. When we persevere, we gradually start to notice that the noises coming from our mouths and entering our ears are not only empty and unnecessary, but meaningless. We realize that it is time to learn another way of communicating: the language of silence.

15

Understanding a New Language

The language of silence is the language of our eyes, feelings, and attitudes. It has a powerful vocabulary that we all use, but most of us aren't aware of it or use it in a negative way. For example, when we are angry or dislike someone, even if we keep our mouths shut, our eyes can take on a critical or even a ferocious look—hence the expression, "If looks could kill . . . (I'd be dead!)." When our attitudes and feelings toward someone are negative, we emit a repelling vibration that they pick up. This kind of energy is often found in workplaces and relationships where issues are not communicated verbally and festering discontent creates an atmosphere of noncooperation and heaviness. This inevitably leads to misunderstandings; when we feel rejected or criticized, the mind always focuses on the worst aspects and actions of those we feel are judging us.

Instead of employing the language of eyes, feelings, and attitude in this destructive way, we can try out the positive language of silence. Next time you feel angry or negative toward someone, simply be still and quiet, and contemplate yourself, the other person, and the present moment. This helps us to let go of that negativity and reveals the "grammar" and "tense" of silence. The grammar of silence is simply this:

I AM: Contemplating the "I" of the pure self

You ARE: Acknowledging the existence of the other

Now: Acknowledging the present tense—that we live in the present moment

By tuning in to all three elements, we use the language of silence positively. This language of respect, acceptance, appreciation, and inclusiveness has its truest expression in nonverbal communication, particularly the body language of the eyes and face, for our body language is a reflection of our thoughts, feelings, and attitudes, whereas when we communicate using words, we often camouflage our real feelings and negative attitudes.

Starting Now

You are starting your journey into silence now, and the correct tense for the language of silence is always the present tense, because practicing silence is about being present in each second, in the *now*. When we have an awareness of the present moment, and of the thought created in that moment, we gradually learn to cancel out the past and future and be truly here in the present. Then we can recognize and take the opportunities that life is offering us. Using the language of silence equips us to see this, whereas previously our minds were cluttered with the noise of the past and the future—as overcrowded as a can of sardines! This new language brings with it a new way of seeing and thinking; we find ourselves thinking far less and, with the energy we save as a result, can increase the quality of our speech, actions, and relationships.

So, are you ready to start out on that first step? Then speak to your mind, direct it toward peace and stillness, and simply do not allow it to interfere. The biggest challenge in learning the language of silence is to let go of our innate human compulsion to incessantly think, speak, and do. This simple exercise shows you how to check the mind's noise. By slowly focusing on and remembering the original state of the self and not allowing the mind even one "What?" "Why?" "How" or "Not now!" gradually, and with little struggle or effort, you build inner contentment and a natural release from burden, stress, and wasted energy.

Take a Moment . . . to discover your peaceful soul

1. Stop for a moment or two, and become still and silent. Take the thought "I am a peaceful soul" and hold it in your mind firmly, slowly, and confidently. Whenever you hold one thought in the mind, it gradually releases its energy into the consciousness.

2. While you are holding this thought, other wasteful thoughts will try to butt in. Pay no attention to them, no matter how great the attraction or the force with which they throw themselves at you.

3. Whenever you are distracted, keep returning to the original thought, "I am a peaceful soul."

4. As you come back into the everyday world, try to retain some awareness of great peace.

PEACEFUL THOUGHT
*Now my mind is empty, clear, and ready, and I choose
what and when to think.
I have begun to master my life just with the change
of a thought in one second, the one second of now.*

∞ 4 ∞

LEARN . . . the ABC of silence

PEACEFUL THOUGHT
I am a soul, a point of energy.
I am serene.
I am peaceful.

WHEN WE START LEARNING A NEW LANGUAGE, we go back to basics. It's the same with the language of silence. The ABC of silence comprises three closely linked steps that help to still a confused and restless mind so it can be so still and silent that it absorbs healing energy. Step A is *reflection*, which leads toward step B, *concentration*, and this moves us effortlessly into step C, *connection*.

Step A: Reflection

Effective reflection does not mean fixing your mind on an idea and thinking it over and over again. This just wastes time and energy without nourishing either the mind or the soul. Instead, to settle into blissful reflection, first find your natural inner stillness. When it is hard to find stillness, we often try to focus the mind by repeating a mantra or a series of words over and over. But such forced techniques bring tension to the mind, rather than the freedom of stillness. True reflection and concentration cannot be compelled; they come naturally once you are quiet within.

Step B: Concentration

Once you are still and reflective, try to drift into a gentle and healing state of remembering, reflecting on who you are and contemplating the peaceful soul that you are in essence. Then concentration will come to you, knowing it is welcome. Once you find true concentration, notice how your thoughts become fewer and fewer until, in an eternal moment of reflection and stillness, you reach the point of essence. We might refer to this as peace, the eternal self, or God.

Step C: Connection

The mind can remain at this point of essence, calm and serene. Because it is so focused on the point of its reflection, there is no outward loss of energy, and so the self starts to feel full. Such a concentrated state creates an automatic connection with the self as a spiritual being and with God, the source of being. As the concentrated thought becomes more pinpointed, it "plugs in" to this source of being, and a current of spiritual energy flows from the eternal source to the self. This connection is very loving and brings a special form of energy into human consciousness.

We all receive currents of energy all the time, from other human beings, from matter, and from our roles in life, but these can pollute our innate energy or block its release. The human mind and heart need this nonhuman current of the eternal source, for it creates a different circulation of energy; it creates in us, simultaneously, wonderful feelings of purification and liberation. When this connection is maintained daily, it builds a reservoir of permanent spiritual peace inside that we constantly and quietly share with others, like a flower silently offering its beauty and fragrance to all in its vicinity. Although it does not feel as if it is doing anything, such a connected mind becomes an instrument of the divine.

Take a Moment . . . to connect

1.   Stop for a moment or two, and become still and silent.

2.   Open your awareness and let your attention move beyond sounds, action, tasks, and people to focus on your original state of peace. Connect to that point of essence.

3.   Now, through your point of essence can you find a connection with the source of being, the one who is the infinite ocean of peace?

4.   Absorb that great peace and energy, and try to retain awareness of this connection as you go back into your everyday life.

REFLECTION

God tells us, "Focus on me and I will whisper good things in your mind."
Ego is such that it makes the mind race; it will not allow you to be still.
But, to make the mind peaceful and benevolent, God keeps telling us,
"Focus your mind on me."

—Dadi Janki

∞ 5 ∞

MAKE TIME . . . create the moments you need for silence

PEACEFUL THOUGHT

To create a time of silence takes just a second. A second is a drop of time . . .
a drop of time through which I step to renew myself deep inside.
So I stop, for a second, and say to myself, "Now I shall go inside."
In the space of that second, I pass beyond all the muddle
and find myself in my original state of peace.

HOW DO YOU FIND ENOUGH TIME TO PRACTICE SILENCE during a busy day? It's as easy as establishing an aim. If you have an aim for your journey into silence, that aim creates just the time it requires. This notion—of an aim making time—might seem strange, but aims and time are very closely connected. Aims function on three levels: they are for the moment, as well as for today and for life. If your aim for life is to sustain a good relationship, for example, it involves the daily aim of practicing patience as well as the aim of each moment—to observe what words or actions are necessary or appropriate right now. To clarify what your aims are, try the easy exercise below.

Whatever your aim in using this book, it's best to begin by becoming silent for a second. It's not difficult to find a second to stop, and once you find a second's peace, the experience leads seamlessly to another second, and then another, and soon those seconds have become a minute or even an hour. Each of us can choose when and how long to stay in that time of silence. Every day is full of hundreds of thousands of opportunities for the peace experience. Seconds are ticking themselves into our awareness constantly. How many seconds are there in a day?

Clarifying Your Aims

Now that you have let yourself stop for a second of silence, use that time-out to reflect on your longer-term aims—for today and for life—and to discern which ones should take highest priority. Simply being aware of your next step gives you the energy—and time—to carry out the work required to move toward the desired outcome.

Take a Moment . . . to clarify your aims

1. Stop for a moment or two, and become still and silent. Open your awareness and connect to a state of peace.

2. Now reflect, by asking yourself, "What are my aims?"

3. To apply discernment, try to prioritize your aims, asking yourself which are really important and which to act on first. Write them down as follows:

My aim for the moment is:

My aim for this day is:

At the moment, my life's aim is:

"I go inside and connect with my inner peace. I become quiet, and everything becomes clear: until I believe in myself and stop depending on others' approval, I will always fear what might happen. In this moment I find faith in myself. I accept that it doesn't matter whether others agree with me or not. I find the courage and determination to step forward."

4. Now try to take these feelings about courage into your everyday life.

PEACEFUL THOUGHT

Do I find time or do I create time?
How much time do I need to create silence in my mind?
Once I have decided on the aims of my day,
then there is always the time I need.
I, not circumstances, create the space of time in my day.

∾ 6 ∾

GET YOUR BEARINGS ... know where you can find peace

PEACEFUL THOUGHT

*In quietness I contemplate an egoless self, a self free from wanting,
possessing, and expecting, a self of natural humility, a being of self-respect.
In humility I give space, and in that silent, sacred space,
where "I" and "my" dissolve, a spiritual human being emerges,
perfectly free of sticky dependencies, perfectly capable of trust and
confidence. A new selfhood is created.*

IF YOU CAN DEDICATE A PHYSICAL SPACE to your silent practice, you will find that it becomes more powerful: if you sit daily in the same spot, vibrations of peace gradually build up. Your space becomes full of accumulated peaceful thoughts; then anyone who steps into that place of silence will experience peace and calm, too—and an instant recharging of the mind and body. Of course, you also have to create that place inside you through your practice because the physical space may not always be available. Then wherever you are or whatever you are doing, for a second or two you can step into your peaceful inner space and settle the mind in peace.

A spare room makes an ideal indoor space in which to practice silence. If you can set aside a room that will be used only for your silent time, it will be your oasis, especially if you live in a hectic city or have a demanding workload. Of course, most of us don't have space at home to set aside a whole room for practice. In this case, just select a corner of a room, but try to choose a room that is relatively free of people—even when a busy room is empty, noisy vibrations linger. Try not to choose a bedroom; the vibrations of sleep don't help the mind to stay alert. If you try to practice silence in a sleepy space, you will be less able to concentrate and may even fall asleep! On drowsily awakening, you may think you have made a great connection with peace—or even discovered Nirvana—but to experience the spiritual peace that brings with it a feeling of stability and renewal, you need to remain fully conscious.

If the ideal place is not available, select a neutral space. By spending time there in silence, you will build up positive, peaceful energy in the space. Whether your physical space for silence is a room or a corner, it's best to have the minimum of furniture and, if possible, only a chair or a comfortable cushion to sit on. You might like a CD player or iPod and speakers to play calming music, and a candle or nightlight to focus your attention. Keep the colors in the space pale—cream, white, or any soft pastel color will ensure a feeling of lightness.

Alternatively, you could adopt a quiet spot outdoors as your special silent place. In nature, many places are naturally serene: you could look near the sea, in a wooded area, on a hilltop or cliff, or in your garden or local park. Whichever spot you choose as your silent space, indoors or out, try this simple routine to help you to start building a regular practice:

Simple Silence Routine

1. Go to your silent space. Put on some very soft music to soothe you, and light a candle. Place it so that it is at eye level when you are sitting.

2. Sit in a comfortable position, either in a chair or on the floor supported by cushions.

   First focus on relaxing yourself completely: relax your body, and then let all thoughts of the day slip away.

3. Keeping your eyes gently open, concentrate on the candle's flame. Keep your eyes open to stop you from falling asleep. Try to remain here in silence for ten to fifteen minutes. You might like to use the "relax and release" exercise (next) during this time.

4. When your practice time has finished, close your eyes and have a stretch before getting up carefully. Try to take the experience of silence back with you into the everyday world.

Take a Moment . . . to relax and release

1. Stop for a moment or two, and become still and silent. Open your awareness and connect to a state of peace.

2. Focus on these thoughts by saying them to yourself in your mind:

   "I am a peaceful being, a point of light.

   I am a peaceful soul."

3. To relax your body and mind, slowly repeat the following words to yourself in your mind to promote concentration:

"I relax my thoughts and release the tensions and the difficulties of the day.

I release . . .

I relax . . .

I recharge again slowly.

I release . . .

I relax . . .

I recharge.

I feel peace, freedom, and lightness . . .

peace, freedom, and lightness. . . ."

4. Keep these thoughts in mind until they are so much a part of your awareness that you no longer need to repeat them. If you find your mind drifting, bring it back by saying, "I release . . . I relax . . . I recharge . . . peace . . . freedom . . . lightness." Continue until your period of silence is at an end.

REFLECTION

When someone has been eating some fruit and you come into the room, there is a fragrance of fruit. The fruit does not make an effort to spread its fragrance, but others experience it. In the same way, silence can be experienced in the atmosphere. When we are engaged in powerful meditation, whoever comes into the room can experience the silence in the atmosphere.

So if silence can transform the atmosphere, it can transform matter. In silence not only is the mind transformed, but matter is purified.

—Sister Sudesh

∞ 7 ∞

ANCHOR YOUR DAY . . . know when you can find peace

PEACEFUL THOUGHT
*As I sit quietly, the qualities of my spirit are blooming and
thoughts of joy and serenity glide through my mind, through all of my being.
I remain here in the fullness of this consciousness, released from any other
thought. My only awareness is of my self as a being of completeness,
tranquil and silent. I am forever connected.
I am forever serene.*

FINDING THE RIGHT TIME OF DAY as well as the right place for a silent practice will help you to experience the most silence can offer. The beginning and end of the day are good times to build in a period of silent practice—on waking and before bed. You might also like a short practice in the evening, when you return home from an overloaded day, to recharge the self with silence.

Morning Practice

Sitting in stillness and silence early in the morning lays the foundation for the whole day, providing a spiritual "breakfast" that gives the mind and the intellect energy for the day ahead. Dawn is a very special time of the day for silent practice. If you can, try to practice well before sunrise, when the traffic of human thoughts starts to circulate. At this early hour, there is a strong sense of inclusiveness, of being linked with time and with the divine. The early-morning meditation practiced by yogis is called Amrit Vela, "the Hour of Nectar." In this hour of sacred silence, the soul is able to experience the deepest and most personal connection with the self and God.

Morning practice is particularly effective in quiet places outdoors, since nature seems to extend us an invisible welcome to sit and experience the natural, eternal tranquillity of life. I remember one Christmas morning in Australia when I was about thirteen years old. I decided to go for a short walk in the forest near our home. Dawn was just about to break, and no one else was yet awake. After walking for some time, I sat down with my back against the trunk of a red gum tree to gaze out over the horizon, which was just beginning to be filled with light. About ten yards in front of me was a fir tree; its many slender trunks formed a clump of twigs and branches, like a huge ball with masses of soft, green needles. From each of the needles hung a drop of translucent dew.

I sat quietly against the red gum. Everything was silent and completely still. As I sat, I heard a few birds chirping and some ants scrambling over dry leaves. A cluster of bees started humming and hovering over the heads of some purple flowers, ready to fill their morning bags with purple gold. These natural sounds in that morning silence gave me an incredible sense of peace and a sweet joy. I had stepped away from my "human beingness" and had become a *part* of being, a *part* of this forest scene—quiet, still, not thinking, just there. Then the topaz face of the sun streamed yellow and then pink over the horizon, its light, like invisible fingers, caressing the drops of dew hanging in their thousands on the fir tree. Each drop became a lamp of color—some pink, some mauve, some blue, and some yellow. As the fir tree swayed in the gentle breeze, the colors of each lamp changed from mauve to gold, from pink to blue, from blue to green, from green to red. I had never seen any-thing so beautiful. It was as if nature were displaying her own decorated Christmas tree.

In those moments of revelation in nature, I experienced a quiet ecstasy deep in my heart, far deeper than any joy I had previously experienced. I just wished to remain in that silence and feeling of union, a feeling beyond anything of this earth. The next moment, the dazzling colors melted, the light shone stronger, and the sounds of the forest became louder; the day had now fully started in the forest, and dawn had dis-solved away.

Dusk and Bedtime Practice

Another appropriate time to recharge the self through silence is dusk, when the energy traffic of thoughts slows down, and again before bed. When there is less thought and energy traffic, it is easier to direct our thoughts and experience the subtle connection to God. I was once told by an elder yogi always to go to sleep before the new day meets the old day—before midnight—to keep the mind fresh and active for the fol-lowing day. It reminded me of the Cinderella story, when, at the stroke of twelve, all the heroine's finery turned back into pumpkins, rats, and rags! The elder yogi explained that the human mind and body need to work with the natural rhythms of the day; otherwise, both are pushed into unnatural extremes that make us feel exhausted, restless, heavy, and hazy. Left to follow its natural rhythm, the body—like nature—starts to stir early in the morning and then, at dusk, begins to slow and eventually shuts down to rest.

Going to sleep after midnight on a regular basis upsets the natural biological clock. Even if we then sleep for eight to ten hours, we wake up feeling heavy and tired. When we upset the biological clock, the mind cannot think clearly and the body's rhythms are sluggish—the effect is evident in the symptoms of "city sickness": stress, anxiety, sleeplessness, and mental fatigue.

The intensity of my silent morning experience in Australia was not to repeat itself until many years later, in India—in the heart of "yoga country" on a sacred mountain, similar in myth and significance to Mount Olympus in Greece. In the ashram, we experimented by going to sleep early—at around ten o'clock at night—and waking very early, at around four o'clock the next morning. This early-morning rising proved to be a marvelous experience. We got up, bathed, dressed, and walked silently, guided by the December moonlight, to the large meditation room, where, warmly wrapped in large white shawls, we quietly sat crossed-legged on the floor, not speaking a word or looking at anyone. In the dimly lit room, where about three hundred of us were sitting, there were three benches at the front. Three yogis, all women, sat on the benches facing us, each wearing a white sari and a warm, white shawl.

These women were silently guiding the meditation. They were peacefully gazing at everyone, but their eyes seemed far, far away. I felt a gentle white light emanating everywhere, a light filled with peace and divine presence. It seemed that a magnetic canopy of silence and peace covered the room for the hour that we sat there. I found myself absorbed in a bliss that took me beyond physical reality; I felt a oneness with all things, but particularly with God. For a moment, it brought back the memory of the Australian forest so many years before—the feeling of being beyond, of quiet ecstasy, of joy and oneness—although now the union was with God rather than with nature. My soul was absorbed in a union with divine light, with eternity, and with the unique being who moves all things. You might like to try the following practice in your early-morning sitting:

Take a Moment . . . in nature

1. Sit in a peaceful corner of a garden or park on a calm, still day with your eyes gently open. Breathe slowly and deeply in and out three or four times, allowing your body to relax.

2. Observe the leaves, buds, flowers, stems, and branches. See how still and quiet they all are. As you watch them, allow your thoughts to slow down until they are as still and serene as the garden. Let yourself totally relax.

3. As your sense of inner quietness grows, visualize it flowing through your whole body, cell by cell. Do this breath by breath until your whole body is at peace. Understand that this peace comes from within you.

4. Close your eyes and imagine there is a garden deep inside you that is always full of peace, harmony, and beauty. This is the spiritual dimension of your being. As you become still and silent, this inner garden flourishes.

5. Remain in your inner garden, allowing your spirit to bloom and allowing your mind to be released from all other thoughts. When you emerge back into the everyday world, take the feeling of tranquillity and serenity with you.

REFLECTION

I use the power of silence in terms of little pauses. I see something, I hear something, and in a pause I remind myself of who I am—I am a being of light—and I remind myself of who you are—you are also a being of light. Then I don't see the differences of external form, but instead see the unity of the inner being and the eternal connection we have. In that connection healing happens.

—Jayantiben

∞ **8** ∞

TUNE IN . . . determine who you are and what you need

REFLECTION

When I change the quality of my thoughts, they become
appreciative thoughts; the comeback of that for me personally is that
I feel very comfortable and content within.

—Jayantiben

THE STILLNESS OF SILENCE HALTS THE MIND and stops the intellect from analyzing and categorizing. This brings moments of clarity, and in these moments we understand our thought processes better—what motivates us and which concepts have conditioned our behavior. As the mirror of understanding comes into focus, we can also see what we need to do or be to develop spiritually.

What Do You Really Think?

In silence, the mind controls thought energy to such an extent that it no longer moves automatically when nudged by habit, and so we are no longer subservient to old patterns of behavior and thinking. Without this stillness, the same old concepts and patterns would feed the mind, resulting in the same old conclusions and barriers blocking any creative breakthrough. Grasp the opportunity now to take a silent moment to examine some of the ideas that have influenced your life so far:

Take a Moment . . . to discover what you think

1. Stop for a moment or two, and become still and silent. Take some time to reflect on your current understanding of one or more of the following words, which describe abstract moral concepts. As you work through the list, other abstract terms may occur to you; consider those, too.

> Reflection
>
> Acceptance
>
> Forgiveness
>
> Happiness
>
> Kindness
>
> Belonging
>
> Respect
>
> Stillness

2. If it is helpful, write down your thoughts about each of these ideas before finishing your period of silent reflection.

Understanding Spirituality

In this state of clarity, now you might like to explore the language of spiritual knowledge as you currently understand it; this is something most of us rarely do, but it can provide illuminating insight into your personality and makeup. Often, such words have become so integrated into our social traditions that they have lost their true meaning or spiritual essence. Discovering the lost essence of some of these terms will help to further your practice and experience of silence. The following exercise will help you to acknowledge the everyday meanings of such words and allow them to dissolve, with respect, before your new understanding blossoms into being.

Take a Moment . . . to discover your own truth

1. Stop for a moment or two, and become still and silent. Take another peaceful moment to reflect on one or more of the following words, which are closely linked with spirituality. Consider the ideas imprinted on your thinking from different sources—such as school, religious leaders, works of literature, or movies:

   Angel

   Paradise

   Time

   Eternity

   Heaven

   Death

   Hell

   Sin

   God

   Truth

2. Now settle your mind on a point of silence and stillness, and looking back at the words, ask yourself which meaning feels true for you right now.

3. If it is helpful, write down your thoughts about each of these ideas before finishing your period of silent reflection.

When we re-encounter a much-used expression after it has been freshly defined, or remember its essence and understand it as totally different from its socially institutionalized and collectively agreed meaning, it is like making a discovery. Such personal clarification and insight often spring from an inner need for truth and arrive to meet the needs of our individual characters, aims, and spiritual journeys. Ultimately, as we simply stop thinking and rest in silence, we allow the truth of what we are searching for to come to us. We have cleared an inner space for ecstatic "Eureka!" moments to burst forth. Such moments of silent illumination uplift us and bring an enormous feeling of contentment and release from the mundane and the negative. There is, instead, only the feeling of having found what we were searching for. Such spiritual illumination creates an immense inner strength and confidence.

PEACEFUL THOUGHT

If I stop for a second, step into silence, and concentrate, my thought can take me beyond time and link me to eternity. In eternity, I, the soul, experience the original goodness of the self and the original permanent goodness of God.
This one second of time, when coupled with one concentrated thought, recharges and rejuvenates me at the level of being. This is how I overcome stress, fatigue, and any form of negativity.
This is the miracle that even a second of time can bring.

∞ 9 ∞

CHOOSE WELL ... decide what's really important

PEACEFUL THOUGHT
To perceive what is appropriate requires discernment, not judgment.

IN THIS CHAPTER, WE EXPLORE THREE TYPES OF KNOWLEDGE—primary, secondary, and unnecessary knowledge—and find out how understanding the differences between them can help us to access and experience the many benefits of silence.

Primary Knowledge

Primary knowledge is as simple as it is universal and can be understood and practiced by anyone at any time. It is concerned with how we know ourselves, how we experience truth, and how we bring about changes that make all our relationships—with individuals and in society—easier and more respectful. Those who have and use primary knowledge are not the cleverest or the most politically powerful individuals; they are the people who create and maintain peace and tolerance.

Some individuals have been living examples of this knowledge; they have shown primary knowledge in action. Christ, Buddha, and Lao-tzu, for example, lived according to their beliefs and transformed others' lives by their example in many practical, positive ways, both in their lifetimes and for generations thereafter. This authentic knowledge endures over time. All were able to take responsibility for the issues in their lives, and though they cooperated with and learned from others—even God— they did not remain dependent on that cooperation. Their sense of responsibility enabled them to translate their ideas, values, and ideals into practical action.

How can we live lives that are more like those of these exemplary individuals who committed themselves to learning, practicing, and serving? We can stay awake, aware that each thought, moment, and breath is valuable and should be used in a worthwhile way. We can listen to spiritual teachings and put them into action. Like these strong individuals, we can stop allowing other people, situations, and habits to provide us with the excuses to compromise or get sidetracked. Instead, we can delve into silence and, once there, look at our spiritual values in order to find the remedy to a problem. Trust and patience play a vital part in the creation of primary individuals. They do not seek a "quick fix" but rather allow time and circumstance to become partners in the search for an appropriate way to apply whatever knowledge they have.

When we get our knowledge on the right track, it returns to this pure and primary state of simplicity and also becomes relevant to and useful in everyday life. Primary knowledge sustains us in times of need, remains clear and accessible, and can be translated easily into real-life situations by all who wish to do so.

Secondary Knowledge

Secondary knowledge stems from primary knowledge, but over time it becomes removed from its essential truths. Followers of the great teachers of primary knowledge, for example, often failed to catch the essence of the knowledge, argued with one another about the teachings, and, before long, created their own theological edicts and creeds. In this way primary knowledge devolved into secondary knowledge, which tends to be overtly intellectual and is characterized by great theories and ideas.

While it is undoubtedly useful, this type of knowledge can interfere with clear thinking and can carry an individual off track. For example, philosophy, theology, and other bodies of specialist knowledge can become distorted and misused, particularly when practiced by arrogant and ignorant individuals. This can lead to significant dysfunction both in the everyday lives of individuals and in society—take, for example, the high level of social problems and the chaotic personal lives of so many in the world's economically better-off countries despite our high-speed information systems and educational facilities. An individual who values primary knowledge—who has awareness of basic truths and lives in harmony with him- or herself and God—is concerned instead with restoring peace and respectful well-being throughout society.

Unnecessary Knowledge

So what is unnecessary knowledge? Too much thinking, too much analyzing, too many books, and too much information. There is a lot of knowledge in the world, but the more knowledge we have access to, it seems, the less we actually know! A common phenomenon is for individuals and societies to clog their minds with unnecessary information and fall into the trap of thinking that they have knowledge. What's the antidote to this? Silent reflection followed by well-judged personal action. Without regular silent reflection, knowledge is not digested and absorbed, but merely accumulated.

Take a Moment . . . to sort out your knowledge

1. At the end of a day, stop for a moment or two, and
become still and silent. Try to recall all the things you
have done or thought about today. Now write them down
beneath one of these three columns:

Primary Knowledge   *Secondary Knowledge*   *Unnecessary Knowledge*

2. Now ask yourself these questions:

*Is the "Primary Knowledge" column the longest? For most
people it will not be.*

*Is the "Unnecessary Knowledge" column the longest? For
most people it will be.*

3. Commit yourself to making the "Primary Knowledge"
column in your life the longest. To see how well you are
doing, repeat the exercise from time to time.

Right Knowledge

Today, primary knowledge is heavily eclipsed by secondary knowledge,
and even more obscured by unnecessary knowledge. So how do we
return human consciousness to its essence—primary knowledge? Silence
is a great catalyst, helping us to disentangle intellectual truth from primary truths, which are actually lived.

All the enlightened leaders gained their personal, primary knowledge
after a period of silence: Muhammad in the cave, Christ in the desert,
Buddha under the banyan tree. Saint Francis of Assisi, Mahatma Gan-

dhi, Socrates, and many other great beings also used silent observation and reflection to stay on track.

These beings were not beguiled by secondary knowledge, no matter how sweet it tasted. They saw through it even when no one else did. Take Sophie Scholl, a young student in Nazi Germany. Together with a group of others at her university, she formed a resistance movement, known as the White Rose, against the authorities. The group wrote and distributed leaflets that explained the Nazi regime's lies and racism. When caught, Sophie defended the right of all people to truth, freedom, and justice until the very end, when a Nazi judge sentenced her and the others to death. Though she was very young, she did not succumb to the propaganda of the Nazi war machine.

There are many more examples through history: in medieval Germany, Martin Luther did not accept the directions of the then hypocritical church, interpreting the scriptures in the way he felt was more authentic to the spirit of Christ's teachings. Florence Nightingale, too, stayed in touch with her essence by keeping to her aim to nurse and serve on war-torn battlefields despite being rejected by her family, friends, and society. All these people observed the events around them and, by reflecting on their position in relation to those events, were able to discern what they had to do. They made their choice.

As well as empowering the self spiritually, silence (in the form of observation and reflection) propels us into action. This action asserts the integrity of values that are essential for both a personal and a collective experience of dignity and happiness. When you're struggling to get in touch with your primary knowledge, use this exercise:

Take a Moment . . . to draw toward primary knowledge

1. When you feel confused or overcome by emotions such as anger or hurt, stop for a moment or two, and become still and silent. According to your present situation, ask yourself, "If I cannot be happy / If I cannot find peace / If I cannot forgive / If I cannot control my anger, then what do I know?"

2. Now help yourself draw toward primary knowledge by asking a new question. Try "What am I?" Or "What is the value of having great thoughts or a great talent if it does not help me in my personal life?" Reflect in silence on this. The answers will bring you back to your primary knowledge. When you go back into your everyday world, try to act on this knowledge.

PEACEFUL THOUGHT

In this moment of silence, clarity comes to me and I know what is meaningful and what is unnecessary.
In this moment of silence, my self knows that it need not rush.
In this moment of silence, my senses let go of all that is superficial, glamorous, and hypnotic.
In this moment of silence, my self connects to my original primary state of being and of knowing.
In this moment of silence, my self is again authentic and free.
In this moment of silence, my soul moves back on track.

∽ 10 ∽

FREE YOURSELF . . . ditch an illusion or two

REFLECTION

Be aware that you are a traveler and a guest in this life. There must be no selfishness. Any desire for respect, name, or fame is selfishness. When a person gets stuck in such selfishness, he or she cannot be truly generous.

—Dadi Janki

AN ILLUSION IS A FALSE BELIEF that we take to be real—so real that we have faith in it and live by it. Illusions deceive us into believing they can make us happy and bring meaning to life. For example, many people believe "the more I have, the more I am"—that achieving prestige, wealth, or position creates value, especially in the eyes of others. Such illusions "drug" us into dependence, especially on the need for approval, which, if not realized, can lead to fear, jealousy, depression, and feelings of rejection. Such illusions impair our capacity to reach the authentic roots of our being.

Reaching our spiritual roots, or original identity, is the aim of silence. But as long as we harbor illusions, our minds will never find peace. By practicing concentrated silence, we can see these illusions for what they are and be liberated from them. One way to start recognizing your own deeply held illusions is to try having a dialogue with the self during your silent practice. As you sit in the quiet concentration of silence, see whether you can tap into a higher or wiser self and ask it some questions.

Here's an example; the conscious mind asks the questions, while the answers come from the higher self:

Q & A Session

Q: Freedom is one of the most important human rights. So why do I so often feel like a prisoner?

A: On a personal level, the greatest barrier to freedom is ourselves. Someone else does not make us angry, does not appreciate us, or opposes or bad-mouths us. How we choose to react to what others do or say determines whether we remain caged or become free. The bars on the cage are our own responses, not the incidents themselves.

Q: Why do I find this idea so difficult to accept?

A: Because we have learned to escape responsibility extremely well by blaming "the other." This "other" could be another person—a friend, relative, boss, even God—but it could also be our state of health, a past incident, some legal restriction, public transport, the weather . . . the list is endless.

Q: Can I break the pattern? Can I become free?

A: If you want it sincerely enough, then you'll quickly recognize the biggest illusion of all and no longer give "the other" the right to cage, manipulate, intimidate, squeeze, control, or own you. Freedom begins with wanting it but is realized only by recognizing when old, ingrained habits are feeding the mind. The key is to start watching the mind.

Q: *How can I watch my mind? My thoughts are so fast, so subtle, and so slippery. Often I am not aware of what is happening until it is too late.*
A: You need to use your third eye—your intellect. Let it observe your mind and old patterns, work out what is happening, and then decide what to do. In this way the intellect checks and then changes the direction of your thoughts until they are more appropriate. It's easy to start. First, decide that this is what you want to do; then take a moment in silence to bring it about.

Becoming Free from Bad Habits

Learning to be quiet is the first practical step in freeing yourself from the illusions blocking your journey to self-realization. When there is too much rush, too much passion, or too much "I-ness" in actions, we become mentally bloated. This can lead to such unhelpful negative habits as confusion or an explosive temper. Through silence we can stop the overtalking, overthinking, overdoing, and over-the-top emotions. This works because silence frees the intellect to do three things: to observe, to discern, and to choose. As the third eye, or intellect, observes, it notices that from the inner upheaval of stress, anger, or fear, silence and stillness can restore inner peace. As it discerns, the intellect equips us to step back and notice the negative thoughts lying behind the stress, anger, or fear. Finally, the intellect allows us to wield the most powerful weapon in the battle with negativity—the power of choice—as we consciously choose not to be triggered into unhelpful emotional states by negative memories and word or thought associations. Thus, these three processes gradually liberate the mind. See how it feels by trying this exercise. If practiced regularly during the day, it does wonders for the health of body and soul.

Take a Moment . . . to check and change

1. Stop for a moment or two, and become still and silent.

2. As you become quieter, notice how your third eye, or intellect, comes into focus. You may experience this as a sudden ability to see better or as less blurred vision, as everything becomes transparently clear.

3. Now that you have greater inner peace, notice how your intellect allows you to identify the negative thoughts behind your anger or fear. Think about how these thoughts are not you and not the thoughts that you want. When you no longer identify with such thoughts or get absorbed in them, the energy you were losing because of them ceases to drain away.

4. Now exercise the power of choice. Choose to think differently and make an affirmation to yourself. You might say, "I choose now to be quiet and peaceful," or "I no longer choose to follow old patterns or act on old memories that trigger negative reactions." If your decision is firm enough, your thinking track will change.

REFLECTION

Many people ask me, "Where do you receive your power?" I reply, I have many sources of energy but no source of energy drainage. I don't have any unnecessary expenditure. Let me just continually create and share that with others. Let me remain full of happiness, peace, and silence. Energy comes from doing right actions. Selfish actions create drainage.

—Dadi Janki

❧ 11 ❧

GET HEALED . . . silence that anger

PEACEFUL THOUGHT
Through a second of time, a drop of silence,
I build a bridge to eternity and bathe in the peace of the ocean.

HAVE YOU EVER BEEN ANGRY, then walked to a calm place in nature—maybe to a lake or the ocean shore? Remember how your anger just dissolved and melted away? This is because water has a cooling, soothing effect on the physical body and the emotions. After a little time in such a calm spot, the soul feels healed. What good fortune, then, if you are lucky enough to live by a river or the sea! But if you live and work in the heart of the city surrounded by concrete, you can't just run away to cool off by the river when you feel anger rising. Where do you go? The best place to retreat is inside your self; go within and you will find a very similar healing space. This is because anger is just superficial. When you move deeper and deeper into silence, you drop below such superficialities and find a place of peace. Try the exercise at the end of this chapter to see how, in just a minute, you can easily go inside and connect with that healing peace. Becoming silent starts to create the thoughts that take us within, and when we change the quality of our thoughts, the peace we find is able to remove the heat of negativity.

More than Anger

This technique works equally well to diffuse all the other negative forces that influence us from time to time: jealousy or envy, ego and possessiveness, attachment to things, fear and insecurity. There's a long list, but each one creates a sense of discomfort and inner unease. By practicing silence, we can connect instead with goodness, truth, love, and joy. These positive qualities are within all of us, and as we contact them, they transform negative experiences into something not only positive, but very beautiful, so that we can act in a new and different way.

Indeed, when anything negative comes to mind, by going into silence we can discover its antidote—or the quality at the other end of the emotional spectrum. From fear we discover confidence; from bad thoughts we can tap into the good within. We have within us the antidote to all negative qualities, including the fire of desire fanned by the materialist society we live in. In a world of "I want this and I want this," we can never be content, still, and quiet inside because there is always another shopping list or another item to attain on an external level.

Some might argue that silence just forces us to sit passively and stagnate, to never achieve or get our tasks done. But it does not. Silence allows us to appreciate what we already have, to express gratitude for our own fortune, and to understand that we already have so much that we can and would like to share. From a discontented state of feeling needy and full of desires, silence guides us easily to contentment and generosity.

Experiment with silence the next time you feel angry, discontented, or needy, and let it show you the richness of the treasures that already lie within you. There is an expression—"Silence is golden"; it means that the experience of silence is so beautiful that it shines like gold. We can all dig into that treasure store by using the right thoughts and right understanding, and by going inside. Then we can experience a silence that is sweet, deep, and full. In silence you transform the negative into the positive by connecting with the deepest treasure within.

Take a Moment . . . to diffuse negativity

1. When you feel anger or another negative feeling, stop for a moment or two, and become still and silent.

2. Focus your thoughts on the world inside. Watch them as if they were a movie playing on the screen of your mind. As you watch them, notice how the speed of your thoughts slows down.

3. Out of all those thoughts, select just one—the thought of peace. Hold it in your mind and begin to feel that peace. Understand that peace is your natural state. Peace lies within you. It is who you are. Repeat to yourself, "I am a being of peace."

4. Maintaining this awareness of peace, visualize it spreading into the room, out into the city, and finally throughout the world. Come back to the awareness of where you are, and take the experience of peace out into your everyday life.

REFLECTION

We do not give in order to show off to others, but with wisdom. One who is wise uses everything in a worthwhile way. Give what you have, and more will definitely come. Donate, and you will feel happy. One who is generous is very compassionate.

—Dadi Janki

❦ 12 ❧

DETOX . . . time to cleanse, soften, and stretch

REFLECTION
Silence power is like a fire; it burns all the rubbish.
—Sister Sudesh

WE NOW KNOW HOW SILENCE CAN HELP US to fight the battle against repetitive patterns of damaging thoughts, negativity, and the loss of energy they bring about. But silence can bring us fully into balance with ourselves and help us achieve harmony with others only if the heart, too, lets go of those bad feelings. In this chapter, we look at how to achieve this through a detoxing spiritual "fast" and practical exercises to encourage a more forgiving and respectful attitude.

What are the symptoms that the heart needs a detox? A feeling of bitterness that erupts without warning, especially when triggered by past wounds. A sensation of breathlessness or tightness around the heart brought on not by physical causes but by fear, disappointment, or the pressure of social engagements—this may stem from lack of confidence or past negative experiences. If you recognize any of these symptoms, you would do well to start on this heart-cleansing fast straightaway!

Your Cleansing Fast

This fast is a detox for the mind, intellect, and heart. In the English language, the word "fast" has three meanings: abstinence, or to abstain (from some or all food and drink); moving very quickly; and not fading, or "holding fast." Spiritual fasting encompasses all three meanings; all are necessary to cleanse, strengthen, and heal the mind, intellect, and heart. Though we call this exercise a fast, it doesn't require total abstinence, just abstaining from attitudes and feelings that injure health and well-being, replacing them with beliefs and responses that nurture a pure mind and a happy heart. As in all fasts, emphasis here is on the things we must refrain from—like the sweets and rich foods we abstain from in a body fast—and on the things we must do more of to strengthen the system—think of these as the nourishing fruits and vegetables and purifying water of a dietary fast—so that we emerge feeling cleaner, clearer, and full of positive energy. It's so simple to start this fast: just do less of the items on the first list below and more of the items on the second list.

Things to refrain from:

- For the mind: wasteful and unnecessary thoughts that make it feel clogged and heavy

- For the intellect: arrogant cleverness that blinds us to simple truths

- For the heart: resentment, anger, blame, and obsessive brooding on supposed wrongs, injustices, and wounds

Things to do more of:

- For the mind: frequent periods of silence throughout the day

The fast of silence, especially stillness, diminishes the mind's constant chatter and obsessive stockpiling of opinion. In silence, there is movement of thoughts and feelings while the processes of reflection and observation occur. But in stillness—the highest point of silence—there is no movement of thoughts and feelings, just absolute awareness and concentration.

- For the intellect: more humility

This not only stops us from bingeing on arrogance and misunderstanding; it gives us the strength to create the space into which new, nonjudgmental perspectives can emerge. Without plenty of humility in its new diet, the old, heavy ego, fed by years of habit, takes over again. An egoless intellect keeps itself clear, perceptive, and tuned in to reality.

- For the heart: more kindness

This is the best "juice" for the heart to drink during its fast from arrogance. From the miraculous energy of kindness, we absorb the spiritual vitamins of forgiveness, respect, patience, generosity, and compassion.

Stretching the Heart

On a fasting regime, it is helpful to do some "inner stretching." Practice the following heart-stretching exercises when you are not feeling upset or stressed, so that you have them at your fingertips when any of life's heart-bruising occasions arises.

The first exercise is useful when someone has disappointed you and you feel sad, angry, or frustrated. The second exercise may help when you feel that you've been bad-mouthed or when you feel shaken by critical words. The final exercise is useful when someone misunderstands your motives and you feel that you have to justify your actions or words.

Heart-stretching exercises put a stop to any hardening in the heart and bring about a greater sense of tolerance and ease. They are helpful for enlarging the "spiritual heart": softening any emotional hardness while enhancing your ability to be versatile and opening you to others and new experiences. This softening element is vital. Unless we learn to be more tolerant and accommodating—to mold and adapt—our hearts will remain closed and negative. Then life will be full of fear, blame, prejudice, that modern villain emptiness, and its sidekick, depression.

Take a Moment . . . to counter frustration

1. When you feel anger and frustration building up, stop for a moment or two, and become still and silent.

2. Do not hold on to the bad feelings; instead visualize or feel yourself—your mind as well as your body—stretching as far as you can. Stretch far and wide, past the anger. Stretch right on beyond the frustration.

3. As you open fully into that stretch, repeat the following words silently to yourself:

   "Let it go; it doesn't matter. Just let it go. Let it be."

4. Take this calmness and insight into your everyday life.

Take a Moment . . . to counter criticism

1. When you feel shaken by harsh words or criticism, stop for a moment or two, and become still and silent.

2. Do not hold on to the bad feelings; instead visualize or feel yourself—your mind as well as your body— stretching as far as you can. As you stretch wide, past the hurt, bewilderment, or resentment, remember who you are. Think about the best in yourself. As you stretch and reflect, notice that you feel stronger and stronger.

3. When you feel strong enough and far removed from the criticism, examine the words with a sense of detachment. Is there some truth in the criticism? If so, there's no need to worry or lose any self-respect. As you open fully into your stretch, repeat the following words silently to yourself:

"They've got a point. I'll make sure I fix it."

4. Try to take this calmness and insight back into your everyday life.

Take a Moment . . . to counter misunderstanding

1. When someone clearly misunderstands your intentions and you feel yourself being drawn toward argument and angry justifications, stop for a moment or two, and become still and silent.

2. Do not hold on to the bad feelings; instead visualize or feel yourself—your mind as well as your body— stretching as far as you can. As you stretch wide, beyond the arguments and past any anger, repeat the following words silently to yourself:

"Let it all go. Just let it be."

3. As you hold the stretch, open your mind and try to understand why the other person has misinterpreted your thoughts or actions.

4. Try to take this calmness and any insight back into your everyday life.

Moving and Holding Fast

To grow, improve, and function effectively, we need to move forward, and sometimes we have to do it fast. In this program, there is no time to dillydally; there is only the time it takes to decide and do. When we undertake this fast and these exercises, we quickly eliminate emotional toxins, such as fear, anger, resentment, hesitation, and attachments, and replace them with courage, confidence, enthusiasm, and forgiveness. The speed of change doesn't feel rushed or stressful because we don't allow our time or thoughts to be dispersed, and our spiritual development progresses at a healthy, stable rate. Everything is done without the pressures that blur clarity and purpose.

If our inner base is firm, not only do we move fast without stressing ourselves, but the lessons hold fast. This program of inner fasting and stretching creates a stable inner base, and the colors of kindness and tolerance, for example, no longer fade quickly because of negative circumstances or people. Life holds fast to its own truth, no matter what, and we find we have the strength not only to face the unexpected but also to create positive alternatives. When we hold ourselves fast in spiritual awareness, nothing is impossible.

Maintaining the New You

So, you feel renewed and energized by this spiritual detox, but how do you keep it up? To keep your connection to the source "clean" requires constant work and a vigilant integrity. To prevent pollutants such as carelessness, arrogance, greed, narcissism, or dogmatism from getting mixed up in this spiritual link, work on building humility and honest friends.

REFLECTION

The power of silence is that your heart is very clean. The water of knowledge cleans your heart, and silence is a clean heart and cool mind.

—Sister Sudesh

ೲ 13 ೲ

SILENCE THE SENSES . . .
with generosity

REFLECTION
I will speak sweetly.
I will speak with love.
I will speak less, and I will speak with honesty.
—Dadi Janki

WHEN WE ARE EXTROVERTED WE CREATE A GREAT DEAL OF NOISE and absorb a huge amount through our eyes, ears, and nose. Our physical senses constantly collect and absorb information, which can lead to emotional overload. In order to reap the benefits of inner silence, we need to shut down the senses. This creates a more peaceful state of mind and leads toward introspection. The state of introspection creates deep silence within.

In this silence, we can use our senses to connect with the source of benevolence; silence becomes a channel through which God fills the soul not only with peace and happiness, but also with love. Generosity is one of the purest expressions of love, and when that generosity is spiritual and unconditional, we can go back out into the world and use our senses in a respectful way to add positively to the lives of others. This chapter is based on the reflections on generosity of the great practitioner of silence Dadi Janki.

A Generous Tongue

The tongue works as a needle or scissors. A sweet voice can bind and mend the hearts of others, while harsh words can hurt or even break another's heart. The words we speak must be filled with blessings and good wishes. When we receive blessings from others, we gain the power to progress through whatever lies ahead.

But how do we achieve a sweet voice? Human beings talk the whole day long—just listen to the way you talk to yourself in your mind. Just as, when we speak, the voice echoes, so it is with subtle thoughts—they reach others. Indeed, we often speak more with the mind than with the lips—the mind has a deep connection with our words and actions. The secret to having control over your words and actions, then, is to become peaceful, have self-respect, and remind others of their own self-respect; then all your words will be sweet and well considered.

It's easy to fall into the habit of criticizing others. But if you defame someone or agree with someone who defames another, there will be consequences. The one who sows the seed of defamation receives the fruit accordingly. So be aware and cautious. Anger also makes the tongue bitter. We can remedy this by remaining aware of God; this makes the tongue very sweet! Fill your words with significance, benevolence, and thoughts of service. Otherwise, there is no need to speak! Aim to speak less and do more so that others see that you show by doing.

Sometimes the mouth is quiet but the eyes or lines on the forehead reveal a lack of peace within. The face is the index of the mind. Simply turn within, and you will find that a powerful silence will emerge as you begin to see yourself as a soul and those around you as souls, too.

A Generous Ear

Just as we can train the tongue to talk only when necessary, so the ears, too, can be trained to hear. Nothing wasteful, no matter how small, should enter the ear; it is said that an ant in the ear of an elephant can make it fall. If you hear something about another person, this clouds your perception and affects your thoughts. How do we train our hearing? By developing the ability to listen and absorb only good things. When we absorb the truth, we understand what changes we can make to benefit others.

A Generous Eye

What are the eyes for? To enable us, in silence, to see the world with "soul-conscious" vision. Our physical eyes are very mischievous; it's far better to look at everything with the third eye. Then you see only what is useful, and the actions that follow will benefit yourself and others.

Use your inner eye to look at others' virtues and special talents. Only the external eyes spot defects. When we see the good points in other people, they experience love and happiness. When we tell others about their specialties and virtues, they themselves realize their defects and remove them. Why insult another person? As is our vision, so too is our world. Some people have a very sweet vision, and those feelings show through their eyes and behavior. Whatever we do outwardly can be seen by everyone.

During your silence practice, direct your third eye, too, at God's eyes. God forgives, forgets, and draws us toward him. If someone has very weak eyesight, some quick surgery can help that person to see clearly again. In the same way, God operates on the third eye so that we can see the self, God, actions, and time. Silence is an eye spa for fast surgical operations!

Take a Moment . . . to overcome sensory weaknesses

1. Stop for a moment or two, and become still and silent.

2. To stop yourself from looking for, hearing, or speaking about other people's weaknesses, focus on removing your own weaknesses. Make a list of the things that you commit to overcoming within yourself.

3. Take these thoughts with you and apply them in everyday situations.

A Generous Heart

If you have a generous heart, you will never have wasteful thoughts, use unnecessary words, or be bombarded with extraneous noise. Introspection—which comes from silence—makes our feelings and intentions for ourselves and others good and filled with love. Others automatically sense these feelings. We don't need to move into words. The sound from your heart travels directly to their hearts. Everything happens internally, quietly. The exercise below will help you to explore this.

If you apply these rules of sensory silence to yourself, you create a generous life, and others learn by example. You don't need to tell everyone. Just do good actions motivated by humility, truth, and divinity. Whatever seeds we sow, we receive the fruits accordingly. If we sow seeds that bear thorns, we can't expect to eat mangoes! So engage in such acts of goodness and charity that the results are of benefit not only to yourself, but also to the world.

Take a Moment . . . to understand others

1. Stop for a moment or two, and become still and silent.

2. In the quietness of that moment, ask yourself the following questions:

   - Whom do I need to take the trouble to understand more deeply today?
   - Whom have I rejected in my heart?
   - Whose difference have I not been ready to welcome?
   - Whose sorrow have I not been willing to share?

3. Remember that when you feel mercy, forgiveness, and friendship, your own nature becomes good. Now think of those people and extend those feelings to each one of them.

4. Notice how this makes you feel about yourself, and take these thoughts back into your everyday connections with other people.

REFLECTION

I shall keep my vision for everyone very good.
I shall have feelings of love and mercy for everyone.
All I have to do is create a good atmosphere—
an atmosphere of peace, love, and generosity wherever I go.

—Dadi Janki

∽ 14 ∾

WAKE UP . . . and be attentive

PEACEFUL THOUGHT
Humility opens the heart of the soul, which gives value to others and respects their uniqueness as well as its own.

NOW THAT WE ARE NEARING THE END OF THE BOOK, I include a parable to put all the thoughts we have considered so far into context. I first heard this story many years ago after an hour-long early-morning meditation. The meditation room was filled with a white, almost silky silence and complete peace. Usually, after meditation, we would all get to our feet and return quietly to our nearby homes. On that day, however, the senior yogi, who had been a student of Brahma Baba when she was a very young woman, asked us to stay on for a few moments, since she wished to share her inspirations of the morning.

The senior yogi described a scene in which there was a cage, huge and dark, filled with many birds. The birds were doing different things: some were complaining of the dark, others were indifferent and just sitting there, and still others were praying and asking for something better in life. Suddenly, the door of the cage was opened by the Lord of the Birds—the Lord of Life—who had seen their sorrow and was full of compassion for them. He invited the birds to make the journey to his home, where they could live together in perfect peace and freedom. The birds were so happy to hear this news. Many came out into the light and started flapping their wings, flying and swirling everywhere. They had been in the cage for such a long time that they had almost forgotten that they had wings; in fact, some *had* forgotten all about their wings. While the adventurous birds were flying around, others peered out of the cage door but said to themselves, "How do we know this is not a trick? Who knows what really is out there? Let's go back into the cage; there we are safe." So they stayed inside and continued with their complaints and their prayers. Another small group that had started flying with the large group when it ventured out of the cage now became afraid, for the cage was becoming smaller and smaller as they flew farther and farther away from it. As fear gripped these birds, they, too, decided to return to the security of the cage.

The big group kept flying on in the hope of reaching the home of the Lord of Life. They felt that he was waiting for them and that the reason he had opened the cage door was so that they could reach his home and be with him. As they flew, they saw a beautiful island below them. Most of the flock realized that this was not their destination, indeed, that it was a dangerous place, but some, not listening to their warnings, decided to land there and were immediately eaten by wild animals.

The journey continued, and the flock became smaller as misadventures befell them. One group flew too high and was burned by the sun. Others, who said they were tired, decided to rest on a tree, but they rested so long that they were left behind. Another group did not follow the advice they had been given to keep above the clouds and were caught in a storm and blown off track. Eventually, only eight birds arrived at the Lord of Life's home. On reaching the door, two of the birds said, "This is enough. We cannot go farther. Who knows what is ahead? At least we have reached this far. We are peaceful, and no harm can come to us." So they stayed outside. The others entered by the door but were met by rings of fire that had to be crossed if they wished to reach the inner sanctuary of the Lord of Life. Another two stopped here and said, "After all our traveling, and when we are almost there, the Lord gives us such a harsh test to overcome! We will stay here where we are. Too much is too much. We will admire him from a distance."

Four birds remained, and they flew on though the rings of fire. The rings were placed one after the other to form a tunnel, and the birds had to keep to the center to avoid being burned. This was not always easy because the rings moved about and the birds had to stay very alert. One of the birds started to doubt: "Would the Lord do this to us if he really loved us? Does love test?" As he was thinking this, he was caught in the fire of a moving ring, burned his wing, and decided to return to the door. Another bird saw that the tunnel seemed endless, and so she, too, decided to join the birds gathered at the door.

Now only two birds were left, and they were the only ones to reach the Lord of Life. They weren't the most magnificent of the birds, like the peacock; or the most beautiful, like the hummingbird; or the best of singers, like the nightingale; or the most clever, like the parrot; or the best flyers, like the eagle; or the wisest, like the owl; or the most graceful, like the swan. They were simply a sparrow and a swallow. Who would ever have thought that these two would even make their way out of the cage, let alone enter the sanctuary of the Lord of Life!

The secret of their success was that these two ordinary birds had helped each other—something the other birds had not done. The swallow's ability to dive quickly, closing her wings as she flew, created a current of air that carried the sparrow, whose small wings sometimes became too weak to keep moving. The little sparrow's pure heart and love for the Lord never let him doubt the victory at the end of the journey. He trusted the Lord's love so much that he did not see anything as an obstacle, not even his own small wings. His faith was a great help to his friend the swallow, who, although more capable, sometimes felt that she could not make it.

Finally, they came through the rings of fire and arrived in front of a warm, pure light. Their little hearts were filled with bliss and an inner contentment that only genuine accomplishment can provide. "My friends," spoke the light. "You have come. You are most welcome. Enjoy your home. But where are your brothers and sisters? I invited all of them to come. I knew it would be a difficult journey because you had been in the cage for so long—only your love and trust in me and in each other has given you the strength to reach this home of perfect peace. Now that you know the way and the secret of getting here, go back and guide the others. This time, they will all come."

The two friends felt so blessed and so full of happiness on having reached their destination that they willingly turned back to show their brothers and sisters the way home.

Learning from the Story

The senior yogi shared these thoughts after telling this story: When even one or two wake up and successfully make the journey, they can show others the way to free themselves and become peaceful. We don't have to think, "How will I do that?" When you become free, it just happens. She urged us to go out into the world and become instruments for peace, since all souls have a great need for real peace. Is it time now for you to serve in such a way? When you are attentive to silence, the line of concentration to God is always open; then nothing can trip you up as you set out on your journey to fulfill your purpose. As I was walking home in the early dawn light, the yogi's story reminded me of ideas I had read in a Sufi poem. So, when I arrived home, I reached for a book of poetry by the poet Yunus Emre. His poem, reproduced after the exercise that follows, perfectly captured the experience of that early morning's peaceful silence.

Take a Moment . . . to tune your consciousness to the divine

1. Stop for a moment or two, and become still and silent.

2. Sit comfortably and quietly and for a moment appreciate the amazing nature of your body. Then tune your consciousness away from the body; detach yourself from it so your awareness of your body fades.

3. Find an awareness that you are a being of light. As you sit quietly with this awareness, feel the sacred presence of the divine, or the source of love, truth, and joy. As your thoughts focus on the being of light, visualize yourself surrounded by waves of love filled with truth. This love can heal and remove pain you may have been holding on to. Simply absorb this love. Think of it as an ointment that cools a feverish soul and eases any pain. Notice how nurtured and empowered you now feel.

4. Now feel the love spread out around you and beyond you; visualize the waves of love reaching every soul in the human family, healing and empowering them, too.

5. Hold on to the power of this divine love as you come back to the awareness of the present moment and the world and people around you. Watch how it allows you to connect with others in a new way.

WAKE UP . . . and be attentive

So, when I arrived home, I reached for a book of poetry by the poet Yunus Emre. His poem "Find Perfect Peace" captures the experience of that early morning's peaceful silence.

Take a moment to reflect on poems, music, or art that describes your own perfect peace. By focusing on beautiful words, melodies, and pictures, we can more easily tune our consciousness to the divine. What stories have taught you lessons about yourself? What poems have described the peace you are looking for? What music has resonated with you as an instrument of peace?

❧ 15 ❧

EMPOWER YOURSELF . . . gain strength through spiritual silence

REFLECTION

If my love for others is selfless, then I will not use up all my energy. I have to take from the Source, from above, and then give, letting that love flow out in all directions. I am like a waterfall: the water flows through me and reaches others. If you were able to let love flow from you in this way, you would have a beautiful experience.

—Dadi Janki

SPIRITUAL SILENCE IS GOD'S LANGUAGE and, when the soul learns to use this language, many barriers can be crossed. Such silence is active. In times of chaos and upheaval, it provides us with the wisdom to connect with God and the clarity to act appropriately. Then peace flows out of us to protect, guide, and calm situations and people and to bring about reconciliation and respect.

It is sometimes said that if your consciousness is really connected to God and you have no fear or doubt, the energy aura that surrounds you is like a shield that dissolves negative forces. Someone intending to do you harm may not even notice you; you are not "on their radar." How true is this? We are often easily overcome by fear and panic and so fail to generate this highly positive consciousness, but it does work. When we rise above fear, anger, and revenge, the connected consciousness can do wonders.

A Story of Strength

Brahma Baba was in his sixties when a profound change occurred in his life and he became attracted to solitude, which led to religious revelation. His daughter-in-law, Brig Indra, tells that because of his unorthodox approach to spirituality—he thought of God as a point of light and taught that women could become spiritual teachers and decide for themselves what to do with their lives—some locals in Karachi (a city in Pakistan) decided to have Brahma Baba assassinated. They found out where his room lay within the compound where he lived with the students of the Brahma Kumaris World Spiritual University, and they hired a hit man.

The compound was surrounded by a very high wall and guarded by a small number of women. The hit man, armed with a knife, found a point where he could scale the wall unseen and made his way to Brahma Baba's room. He peered through the window and saw Brahma Baba sitting writing, as was his custom of an evening. He knew that this was his opportunity to kill Brahma.

On recounting this story, Brahma said he had felt a strangeness in the air and knew something was wrong. He looked up to see the assassin with the knife in his hand. He recalled that his thought was, "If God wishes me to continue his work, he will protect me, and, if not, then this is my destiny." As he thought this, he was pulled into a deep silence as powerful rays of light filled with peace enveloped the would-be assassin, who was gradually so overcome that he dropped the knife. As Brahma Baba's eyes met his, the hit man found that he could neither speak nor move. Brahma called one of the young women nearby and, without giving any details, asked her to take the man, give him some tea, and then let him out of the compound through the gate. Brahma's faith and commitment to bringing about change in his society in a nonviolent way enabled him to use the spiritual power of silence to channel divine energy and overcome negativity and animosity.

A Silent Strength

We should respect the personal power that silence can bring us. Through silence, we learn the art of concentration, and then we learn to empower ourselves with peace and spiritual love. In silence, we respectfully use the energy of the mind to link with God, and so we become instruments—lighthouses—of God's peace, love, and light. Very little thinking is required to achieve such personal empowerment. We need only to connect with the spiritual self and its original resources and to link lovingly with God, the source of everything. Keeping only this one thought of connectedness in our awareness, we strengthen the self without being distracted by ego and possessiveness. Gradually, we come to understand that, although we do need to make an effort, all things that are to happen will happen, and they will happen in the right way. A genuine connection with the divine is evident through peaceful and respectful behavior and a selfless generosity toward all things.

PEACEFUL THOUGHT
To keep the integrity of spiritual connection, I keep myself simply as a trustee, knowing that nothing is mine.
I do not talk too much about my attainments; I let them be seen through the way I am.
The way I am is the ultimate expression of the power of silence.

❧ 16 ❧

REALIZE . . . living in silence

REFLECTION

Each of us has specialties. Each of us has our own individual part.
Do not compare or compete: there is no point—
you cannot become like anyone else.
You are who you are—unique.
Take whatever is good inside you and leave the rest.
Now perform such a miracle that God is visible
through your eyes and your heart.

—Dadi Janki

THE UNIVERSE RUNS ON PRINCIPLES that maintain and sustain well-being. If we respect these principles, then everything—individuals, the community, and the Earth—will flourish. Practicing silence helps us to tune in to these guiding principles so that we all live in balance, health, and happiness. At the end of your journey through this book, let's look at these guiding principles that help us to live in the spirit of silence. You can return to these eleven wise thoughts whenever your motivation for silent practice begins to waver.

Principle 1: Live Fully in the Moment

There is little point in entertaining memories that stimulate guilt, regret, or nostalgia. The past is past; it's over, and we must move on. It is possible for all of us to enjoy "moment awareness"; staying conscious of the moment keeps away the ghosts of illusion, in other words, those expressed by "could be," "should be," "could have," and "should have." "Now" always comes into focus if we stop for a moment and become silent and still.

Principle 2: Be Aware of Your Inner Resources

We can always find reasons to complain about and blame external systems—religious, political, or social—and thereby conveniently excuse our own inertia, frustration, and negativity. All external systems are human in origin, so it is inevitable that even when established with the best of intentions, they will be faulty to some degree. However, often the problem itself is *not* the problem. The problem is the *way* we think about and approach difficult behavior or harmful acts. We focus on the problem so much that it expands in the mind and entangles us in negativity, pettiness, and trivia. This entanglement stifles clear understanding: we become so focused on what is wrong that we are blinded to the obvious. When we practice silence, we never focus on a problem but instead consciously make room for alternatives and solutions. By recognizing and using our inner resources, we find positive alternatives to the harsh negativities that are all around.

People who regularly contact their great inner reference bank—through silent practice—and tap into its energy rise above difficulties and find benevolent means to resolve issues. Such people attract similar individuals. They come together, like the fingers of a hand, to accomplish a task. This hand is not clenched to punch, push, or beat, but to hold, touch, heal, and encourage. Those who use the inner, eternal principles as reference points work with enthusiasm and silence, and they radiate optimism into the darkest corner of the deepest negativity. They persevere because their strength gives them the confidence to think, "There is always a way."

Principle 3: Rejoice in Generosity

Generosity is a sharing and giving quality that brings about the natural multiplication of everything. It comes with no obligations because it flows from a state of fullness, completion, and freedom—of abundance. But often we forget to be generous because we fear being diminished, misused, or unappreciated. Many of us have grown up valuing selfishness as a defense to affirm ourselves in a greedy and insensitive world.

But generosity is our natural state. In nature, when a seed is given the opportunity to become a tree, it grows and blooms, creating flowers and fruits year after year in cycles of generosity throughout its life. One seed does not give just one fruit; the tree from one seed produces thousands of fruits for many years. The mother tree also creates many, many seeds each year—all full of life-giving potential, whether in the form of new trees or food for other forms of life. There is no reason why we cannot be as generous as nature. However, first we have to understand that the flow of abundance comes only when we free ourselves from the limited, narrow viewpoint of "I" and "my." Practicing silence encourages us to see beyond the limited "I," inspiring us to share the abundance we endlessly receive.

Principle 4: Learn from Positive Opposites

To complete any task effectively, we need a team of values, each thoroughly fit and capable of carrying out its work successfully. Here, success means achieving happiness, peace, and creativity and fulfilling a sense of purpose. There are a number of such teams that guarantee success. Explore these ideas in your silent practice with the exercise below.

What happens when we don't use the whole team of values to deal with situations and people? Commonly, we recognize the importance and usefulness of one value, then stick to it relentlessly. For example, the quality of determination encourages focus, concentration, and the will to face obstacles. However, if you rely on this quality alone over a long period of time, it may degenerate into rigidity, stubbornness, harshness, or even obsession.

When you practice silence you are more likely to notice signals telling you to use your favorite quality's partner values—in this case, patience and flexibility—to maintain balance and flow in situations and relationships. The wisdom to wait sometimes, rather than be tempted to force, is far more respectful to the people you work and live with. Otherwise, those around you might feel pressured, even frightened, by the hardness of your determination, or become angered or frustrated by your inflexibility. A patient, gentle determination is effective because the balance of opposites maintains the natural harmony and order of things.

Take a Moment . . . to explore positive opposites

1. Stop for a moment or two, and become still and silent.

2. As you move into silence, reflect on the following pairs of qualities and think about what they have in common; consider how they deal with the same issue or aspect of life from different perspectives. How are they complementary?

Detachment and lovingness

Stillness and action

Leadership and service

Stepping in and stepping out

Determination and flexibility

Independence and interdependence

3. Now think about how both halves of one of these pairs of positive opposites could contribute something important to your life. If it helps, write down your observations.

4. Take this insight back into your everyday life.

Principle 5: Value Yourself

When you value your uniqueness, you become strong and free, not bound by success or failure, by your talents and opinions, or by your relationships and past experiences. You are not overly lifted by words of praise, nor do you feel crushed by misunderstandings or dislike.

When you practice silence, you step back from others' images of you and are able to appreciate the value of your unique self. You learn that you have an original value that cannot be destroyed, damaged, or copied, and when you get in touch with this inner blueprint you feel the value of the real you so deeply that self-respect begins to flower. You feel complete. When you have an awareness of your unique self, practice humility to sustain it. Humility allows you to give value to others and to respect their uniqueness alongside your own.

Principle 6: Keep Connected

Our inner world needs to connect with the outer world, or society; otherwise, it is like having a seed that is not planted and so can never flower. Creating and maintaining a bridge between the inner and outer worlds facilitates genuine communication with others and helps us to maintain balance and a happy life.

The external world, with its variety of relationships and situations, stimulates us to renew and re-evaluate our internal world of thoughts, feelings, and attitudes. Without this reflection and rethinking, we can remain trapped in everyday problems, pain, and meaninglessness. If we have the awareness and courage to travel back and forth between the inner and outer worlds often during the day, we become "polished"—attuned and ever more mature—as we translate our inner, eternal principles into daily values. We become catalysts for beneficial and benevolent change, both for ourselves and for others. Practicing silence equips us to retreat from the outside world and use the lessons we meet there as opportunities for reflection and change.

Principle 7: Tune In to Each New Moment

We need to be careful not to get stuck in any formula of "right" and "wrong" conditioned by tradition, social custom, or personal emotion. We create happiness when we move according to moment-by-moment awareness, not according to a convenient formula. By taking a moment to be still and silent during the day, we touch the moment and can see what has to be understood and done.

To perceive an appropriate response requires discernment rather than judgment. Judgments are dangerous; they reinforce mental and emotional barriers. Judgments proliferate when we have a narcissistic attachment to our self and a blind, unthinking adherence to rules for their own sake. Discernment enables us to tune in, feel, and respect the need of a moment; discernment is based on kindness.

Take a Moment . . . to be attentive to the moment

1. Stop for a moment or two, and become still and silent.

2. Look back over your day and ask yourself the following questions:

   • What did you hear that was said to you?

   • What did you overhear as people talked among themselves?

- Did you hear what you needed to remember, and not countless other words and phrases?

- Was there a message for you in the words you heard today?

3. As you reflect—relaxed and gently stretching and softening into the remembered words—notice whether something "clicks" to produce an "Aha!" moment. If it does not come today, the words you paid attention to today will be paving the way for a moment of epiphany to come along very soon.

Principle 8: What Goes Around, Comes Around

Believe it or not, all things return to the creator of a thought, a word, or an action. Whatever we throw out to the universe will rebound, sooner or later. We must, therefore, speak, think, and act with care and, even more important, with respect; otherwise, happiness vanishes as quickly as water poured onto hot desert sand. Silence helps us to take a moment to tune in before we act.

Principle 9: A Stitch in Time Saves Nine

When we recognize a thought or a mistake and, without hesitation or fear, act on it, life gets better. When we refuse to see or acknowledge a negative pattern, no matter how small, the damage inevitably gets worse. Recognition is born from humility, just as courage is born from honesty. How can we develop those qualities? Through practicing silence, which tunes us in to our intuition and our better selves so that we recognize the "Aha!" thoughts we must act on and also clearly see mistakes.

Principle 10: Accentuate the Positive

Someone caught up in trivia, pettiness, and drama lives in a state of constant complaint. Instead of flying in freedom and happiness, such people bind themselves within the cage of their dry, narrow hearts. They also seek similar companions. Remember the old saying "Birds of a feather flock together"? While truth can act alone, falsehood usually needs company—to gossip, to disapprove, to judge, to feel smugly justified, and just to pass the time. When people gossip, they reinforce each other's illusions. It is vital that we avoid developing friendships because of mutual dislike or some other negative belief. While a group may glitter, criticism and the pleasure of putting others down cancel *our* right to happiness. What company should we look for to secure our right to happiness? Try the exercise below to find out whether you are seeking company for the right reason—positivity:

Take a Moment . . . to check your sincerity

1. Stop for a moment or two, and become still and silent.

2. In the quietness of the moment, check your sincerity with others by asking the following questions of yourself:

   - What am I sharing with this person?

   - Why am I saying this?

   - Is this situation enriching or uplifting—or something less positive?

3. Notice your responses. As you check, you will see the correct course of action.

4. Now make your decision and opt for a change that will bring you newness, will make you happy, and will help you to fly. Let nothing stop you as you emerge back into daily life.

Principle 11: Space + Silence = Renewal

The final principle for better living is an equation for balance and well-being that supports all ten previous principles. If you practice only this one, the others will follow. Start by recapping the essentials of silent practice with this exercise:

Take a Moment . . . to renew and refresh

1. Stop for a moment or two, and become still and silent.

2. In the quietness of that moment, turn the mind inward for refreshment, and step into an ocean of calm.

3. In the waves of that calmness, begin to unburden yourself of your negativity and uncertainties. Slip into a place of no thinking, and become still.

4. Take the renewed you back into your everyday life.

PEACEFUL THOUGHT
How do I learn?
I learn by thinking and not thinking;
by analyzing and not analyzing;
by focusing and not focusing;
by leading and not by following;
through sound and silence;
through movement and stillness.
I learn by grasping the links between paradoxes.
I learn by observing and by participating.
I learn by implementing the principle of positive opposites because no
extreme works,
no matter how useful a value or method it has been.
All these ways become the natural means of effective learning because they
create the attitude and perception necessary to tune in to the needs of the
moment, of the other, and of the self.
These natural techniques are primary and at the heart of learning.

Afterword:

PEACEFUL THOUGHT
I am a generous soul.
I offer easily and naturally with no strings attached,
and so I feel constantly full.
Nothing ever runs out for a generous soul.
My supply line is unlimited because I am not interested in the process of
counting and measuring what is given.
Well-being is always available to me—and to those who come to me.

WHEN WE FIND SILENCE, IT BECOMES OUR BREATH, and when we use
it effectively, it brings newness and direction to life. Silence con-
quers the tyrants of habit that oppress, suppress, and deceive us.
Silence opens our eyes and ears to see and understand, and thus,
we can overcome all tyranny, because the power of silence gives us
the motivation and the will to become free. Through silence we
can transform confusion into clarity, anxiety into trust, blame into
responsibility, and bitterness into forgiveness. . . . The alchemy of
silence is unlimited.

As each person is unique, so is his or her journey into silence. Of
course, there are deep rivers to swim and huge mountains to cross,
but the heights we reach are all worth the effort. Since we journey
as students, we enjoy the learning, no matter in what form it comes,
because we recognize that exploring and practicing silence is inspi-

rational, challenging, and revealing. Whenever you falter on the path, try this simple practice, which brings you back to the essence of silence:

Take a Moment . . . to journey inward

1. Let the body sit comfortably, and feel it relaxing. Once the body is comfortable, the mind can be set free.

2. Take your mind inside and visualize a spark of light—a point of concentrated energy—in the center of your forehead.

3. As you focus on this spark, think of your spiritual identity as a being of light. Maintain this awareness, and imagine the light shining and rays of peace reaching out into the world.

4. When you are ready, come back to the reality of the world around you, but continue to be aware of the light that is always shining within you.

PEACEFUL THOUGHT
*Every day, I remember to be quiet and to
absorb silence into my everyday life.
I find my time and place, and I am there for myself, every day.
I hold true to my commitment to myself and my practice of silence, so that
my spiritual energy never dwindles and dies.
Every day, I give time and space to sustain my silence so that I shall
experience the renewal that will never cease.*

Works Cited

Brahma Kumaris World Spiritual University. "Brahma Baba." http://www.bkwsu.org/whoweare/brahmababa.htm.

Capra, Fritjof. *The Tao of Physics: An Exploration of the Parallels between Modern Physics and Eastern Mysticism*. 3rd ed. London: Flamingo, 1992.

Emre, Yunus. "Find Perfect Peace." Translated by Taner Baybars. Wisdom Portal.com. http://www.wisdomportal.com/Peace/YunusEmre-Peace.html.

About the Brahma Kumaris World Spiritual University

http://www.bkwsu.org

International Headquarters
P.O. Box No. 2
Mount Abu 307501
Rajasthan
India
Telephone: (+91) 2974-38261 through 38268
Fax: (+91) 2974-38952
E-mail: abu@bkindia.com

International Coordinating Office and Regional Office for Europe
and the Middle East
Global Co-operation House
65-69 Pound Lane
London NW10 NHH
United Kingdom
Telephone: (+44) 208 727 3350
Fax: (+44) 208 727 3351
E-mail: london@bkwsu.org

Regional Offices

Africa
Global Museum for a Better World
Maua Close, off Parklands Road, Westlands
P.O. Box 123, Sarit Center
Nairobi
Kenya
Telephone: (+254) 20-374 3572
Fax: (+254) 20-374 2885
E-mail: nairobi@bkwsu.org

Australia and Southeast Asia
78 Alt Street
Sydney, NSW 2131
Australia
Telephone: (+61) 2 9716 7066
Fax: (+61) 2 9716 7795
E-mail: ashfield@au.bkwsu.org

The Americas and the Caribbean
Global Harmony House
46 South Middle Neck Road
Great Neck, NY 11021
United States
Telephone: (+1) 516 773 0971
Fax: (+1) 516 773 0976
E-mail: newyork@bkwsu.org

Russia, the Commonwealth of Independent States, and the Baltic Countries
2 Gospitalnaya Ploschad, Building 1
Moscow—111020
Russia
Telephone: (+7) 499-263 02 47
Fax: (+7) 499-261 32 24
E-mail: Moscow@bkwsu.org

Brahma Kumaris Publications

http://www.bkpublications.com
enquiries@bkpublications.com

89

Index

About the Author

ANTHONY STRANO has been practicing and teaching with the Brahma Kumaris World Spiritual University for nearly thirty years. Born in Australia, he has lived in Italy, Hungary, Turkey, and Greece; he is currently based in Athens. He travels internationally, conducting lectures, workshops, and seminars on the practical application of spiritual ideas.